BRIGHT IDEA BOOKS

DAYA

by Martha London

CAPSTONE PRESS
a capstone imprint

Bright Idea Books are published by Capstone Press
1710 Roe Crest Drive, North Mankato, Minnesota 56003
www.mycapstone.com

Library of Congress Cataloging-in-Publication Data
Names: London, Martha, author.
Title: Daya / Martha London.
Description: North Mankato, Minnesota : Capstone Press, [2020] | Series: Influential people | "Bright Idea Books." | Audience: Grade 4 to 6. | Includes index.
Identifiers: LCCN 2018058408 (print) | LCCN 2018059403 (ebook) | ISBN 9781543571479 (ebook) | ISBN 9781543571349 (hardcover)
Subjects: LCSH: Daya, 1998---Juvenile literature. | Singers--United States--Juvenile literature.
Classification: LCC ML3930.D29 (ebook) | LCC ML3930.D29 L66 2020 (print) | DDC 782.42164092 [B] --dc23
LC record available at https://lccn.loc.gov/2018058408

All internet sites appearing in back matter were available and accurate when this book was sent to press.

Editorial Credits
Editor: Claire Vanden Branden
Designer: Becky Daum
Production Specialist: Melissa Martin

Photo Credits
Alamy: Everett Collection Inc, 12–13, Paul Froggatt, 15, Zuma Press, Inc., 22; AP Images: Charles Sykes/Invision, cover; Newscom: John Nacion/starmaxinc.com, 5; Rex Features: Amy Harris, 8, Jim Smeal, 20–21, Steven Ferdman, 6; Shutterstock Images: Checubus, 11, Debby Wong, 19, Estrada Anton, 31, Karl_Sonnenberg, 25, Kathy Hutchins, 16–17, 26–27, 28

Design Elements: Shutterstock Images

Printed in the United States of America.
PA70

TABLE OF CONTENTS

CHAPTER 1

SINGING WITH a Message

Daya stands in the center of the stage. Bright lights flash. In front of her is a crowd of people. They cheer when the music begins.

Daya stands with a microphone. A light show plays behind her. Her name flashes on the screen. The song starts slowly. She wears a long white robe. Her hair is short.

Daya rose to fame quickly after high school.

Daya sometimes moves across the stage during her performances.

The song gets faster. Daya takes the microphone out of the stand. She marches across the stage. The crowd waves at her. She shakes people's hands while she sings. She asks the fans to sing with her.

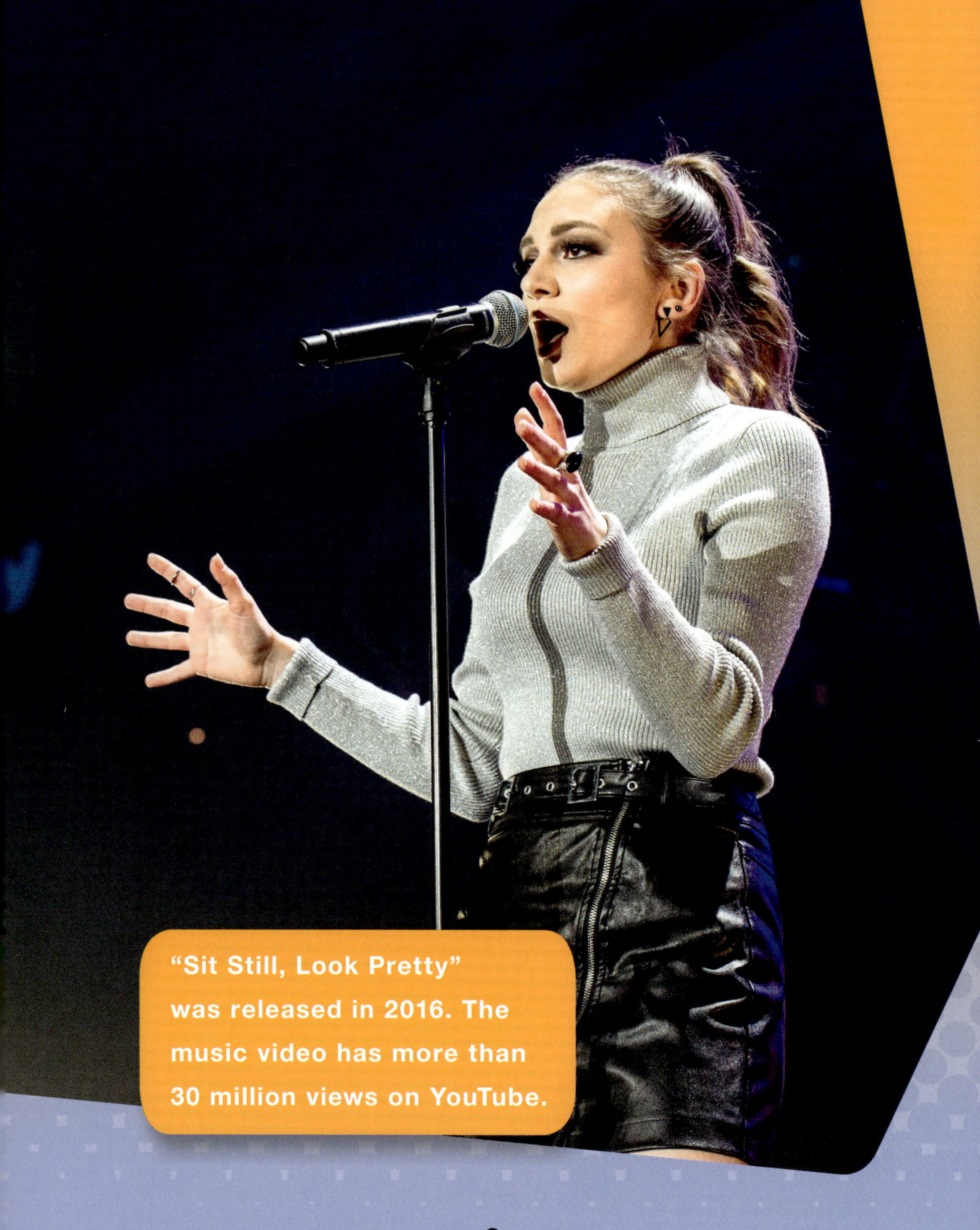

"Sit Still, Look Pretty" was released in 2016. The music video has more than 30 million views on YouTube.

MAKING A DIFFERENCE

Daya has a message for the crowd. She wants everyone to feel like they have a voice. She is only 20 years old. But she is making a difference. She wants girls to feel strong. Her song, “Sit Still, Look Pretty” is about taking charge. Daya wants girls to know they can do anything.

CHAPTER 2

GROWING Up

Daya was born in 1998. Her real name is Grace Tandon. She was always interested in music. She started playing the piano when she was 3 years old.

Daya is from Pittsburgh, Pennsylvania.

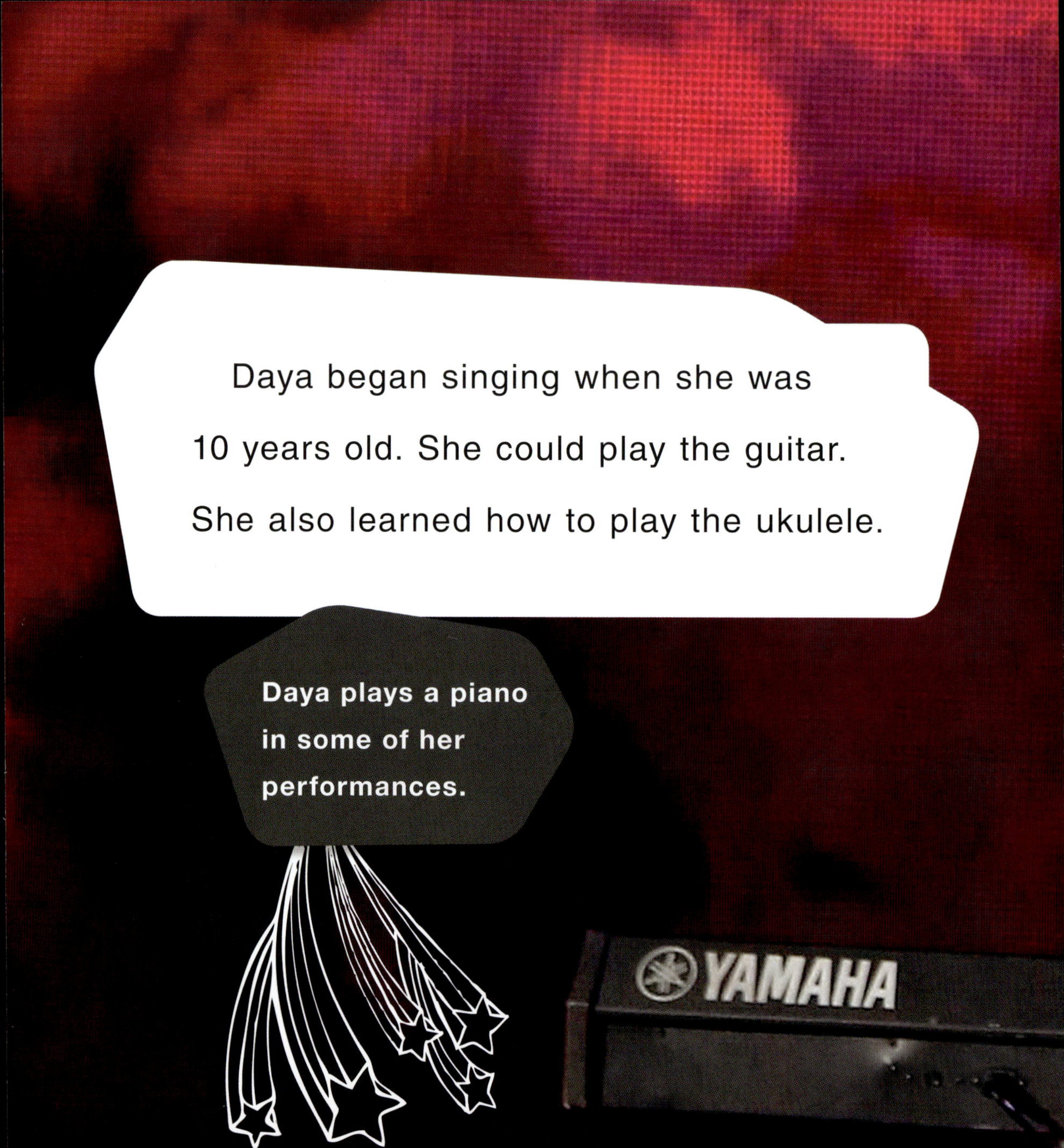

Daya began singing when she was 10 years old. She could play the guitar. She also learned how to play the ukulele.

Daya plays a piano in some of her performances.

MOTIF XF8

Daya says she was a regular teenager. She went to high school. She hung out with friends. Then she started taking classes online when she was 16. This gave her more time to work on her music. Daya's parents supported her dream.

Daya had a lot of practice singing in front of people.

Daya is proud of her family roots.

"DAYA"

Grace decided to go by the name Daya for her career. She chose that name for a reason. "Daya" is the **Hindi** translation of Grace. She chose it to honor her family.

Daya's grandfather is from New Delhi, India. Daya is one-quarter Indian.

CHAPTER 3

HIT Songs

Daya made a short **album** in 2015. She was only 17 years old. There were only six songs on the album. "Hide Away" was one of the songs. It became popular on the radio.

"Hide Away" was released on April 22, 2015. Daya sang it in Times Square on New Year's Eve in 2015.

Daya (center) became good friends with Andrew Taggart (left) and Alex Pall (right) after they made "Don't Let Me Down."

Soon a famous band called her. They wanted to work together. They created the song "Don't Let Me Down."

The song became a hit. It has more than 1 billion views on YouTube. Daya and the band later won a **Grammy Award** for the song.

Daya first made the Billboard Top 100 list in 2016.

Daya released three songs in a year. All of them made the Billboard Top 40. This was a huge accomplishment.

Then Daya was ready to make a full-length album. She started to work with the record company Interscope in 2017.

THE BILLBOARD TOP 100

The Billboard Top 100 is a list of the top songs in the United States. It is put out each week by *Billboard* magazine. The top 40 songs are some of the most successful on the list.

CHAPTER 4

STANDING UP for Others

Daya says she was lucky to have such great parents. She knows not all parents are supportive. Daya's parents were so helpful with her music. Daya wants to help people too.

Daya believes in standing up for others. She thinks the rights of girls and women are very important. She wants to spread this message to younger listeners.

When Daya makes a song, she wants it to have a positive message for young fans.

Daya wants to show everyone that they can be confident with who they are.

Daya writes her own music. Her songs are often about girls taking charge of their lives. Daya enjoys connecting with her fans through her music.

AGE DOES NOT MATTER

Daya thinks everyone should have a voice. It does not matter how old they are. Young people can speak their minds. They can stand up for themselves.

GLOSSARY

album
a collection of songs by a musician

Grammy Award
an award that honors the best artists in music

Hindi
a language spoken in the country of India

TIMELINE

1998: Grace Tandon, also known as Daya, is born.

2015: Daya's first song, "Hide Away," is released.

2015: Daya's first short album, *Daya*, is released.

2016: "Don't Let Me Down" is released in February.

2016: Daya's first full-length album, *Sit Still, Look Pretty*, is released.

2017: Daya wins a Grammy Award for "Don't Let Me Down."

2017: Daya signs a contract to work with production company Interscope.

2018: Daya's single "Safe" is released.

HOST AN OPEN MIC NIGHT!

Daya believes in the power of music. She uses her music to make an impact on her fans. Hold your own open mic! Invite your friends, family, and classmates to share their poems or songs, or perform a celebrity's song. Find how music can bring people together.

FURTHER RESOURCES

Want to know about other popular artists? Take a look at these books:

Gigliotti, Jim. *Bruno Mars.* Amazing Americans: Pop Music Stars. New York: Bearport Publishing, 2018.

London, Martha. *Kendrick Lamar.* Influential People. North Mankato, Minn.: Capstone Press, 2020.

Merwin, E. *Beyoncé.* Amazing Americans: Pop Music Stars. New York: Bearport Publishing, 2018.

Interested in having your own music career? Check out these resources for more information:

SFSKids: Compose Music
www.sfskids.org/compose

Walker, Carolina. *You Can Work in Music.* You Can Work in the Arts. North Mankato, Minn.: Capstone Press, 2018.

INDEX